How to Read and Pray
THE CHRISTMAS
STORY

Marilyn Gustin

LIGUORI
PUBLICATIONS

One Liguori Drive
Liguori, MO 63057-9999
(314) 464-2500

Imprimi Potest:
James Shea, C.SS.R.
Provincial, St. Louis Province
The Redemptorists

Imprimatur:
Monsignor Maurice F. Byrne
Vice Chancellor, Archdiocese of St. Louis

ISBN 0-89243-571-2
Library of Congress Catalog Card Number: 93-78431

Copyright © 1993, Liguori Publications
Printed in the United States of America

Scripture quotations are taken from THE NEW AMERICAN BIBLE WITH REVISED NEW TESTAMENT, copyright © 1986, AND THE REVISED PSALMS, copyright © 1991, by the Confraternity of Christian Doctrine, Washington, D.C., and are used with permission. All rights reserved.

Clip Art of the Christian World, copyright © 1984 by The Order of St. Benedict, Inc. Published by The Liturgical Press, Collegeville, Minnesota. Used with permission .

Cover and interior design by Myra Buechting

Contents

Introduction

Is any story about Jesus dearer to our hearts than the Christmas story? No doubt each of us has our personal favorite. And, of course, everyone loves the story of Jesus' passion and resurrection. But the Christmas story touches a place in many of us that is rarely opened.

Somehow, at Christmas time it's all right to be a child again, kneeling in wonder before the mystery of the manger. It's all right to be amazed at an indescribable star, at angels in the sky, at exotic magi worshiping a newborn baby. It's comforting to imagine ourselves in the warm light of a stable, marveling at this little child. At the crib we can forget for a moment the complexities and the anxieties of our lives.

Perhaps its childlike quality is what draws us to the Christmas story. And—just maybe—that's partly what God, the Author of biblical inspiration, intended the accounts of Jesus' birth to do. Precisely because the Christmas story touches a simpler place within us, God may act within us at this season in a purer way than at times when we are not so open, so simple.

Still, a childlike opening to wonder is not all that is intended by the gospel stories of Jesus' birth. In reality, if all we knew about Jesus was what we learned in the birth stories, and if we knew how to read them for every single implication, we could experience a summary of the Good News. This, too, is the purpose of these stories: they not only open us to a quiet space of soul, they fill that space with truth.

Perhaps because of the very simplicity inspired in our hearts by the Christmas story, many people are put off by scholarly attempts to study it. That was my initial reaction, too. Scholarly analysis, I thought, would distance me from the Lord instead of drawing me nearer at Christmas.

Happily, that distancing did not happen. On the contrary, all of Scripture offers many levels of meaning. If we approach the Christmas story with open hearts *and* attentive minds, it will become deeper, stronger, lovelier than it has ever been before. We will lose nothing from pondering the results of scholarship. We can still approach the manger like a child. We can still love the angels and the magi and the star and all the rest precisely because they will mediate *more* of truth, more of love, than they did before.

You, too, may want to deepen your relationship with Christ through the story of Christmas, even though you may resist the rational questions of scholarship. Yet the effort of working with those questions in awareness of faith will reveal to you the deeper aspects of the story. And those deeper aspects in turn will allow your Christmas simplicity to open you to more of the truth.

This book will not flood you with technical scholarship. You will not be asked to throw away your heart. You will be asked to think and to think patiently. I promise that if you bear with the questions and pray through the suggestions offered, by the time you come to the end of the book you will enjoy an expanded understanding. Certain of your opinions may have changed and *both* your love of the Christmas story and your love of God in Christ will be stronger.

So let's plunge in with confidence.

The Mind of the Writers

Every biblical scholar seeks the deeper meaning of the Scriptures. Most of them do this by trying to discover the "mind of the writer." That is, they try to learn what the writer meant to communicate. That is necessary. The biblical books were written long ago, in another language, another culture. The first readers of these books were interested in different questions and answers than we are, and they emphasized different concerns.

Yet we must not forget that the writers of Scripture were not writing "on their own." They were inspired people who wrote under the guidance of the Spirit of God. This has two implications for us.

First, the writers themselves may not have recognized all the implications of what they were putting down. This is not an unfamiliar process. Every poet has something in mind when she or he writes a poem. But an attentive reader may find much more in that poem than the poet thought was there. If that is true for poets, it surely must be true for inspired writers of Scripture!

Second, the Scriptures *as they stand* were intended by the Spirit of God. This is important to us. Yet it is not always obvious because of a certain concept we twentieth-century Westerners often have. We often have thought that *inspiration* meant "objective, factual reporting." Many still think that when we speak of Scripture as the word of God, we are affirming that it is historically, factually accurate.

But this is the meaning of the phrase "inspired word of God." Inspiration refers to the *meanings* conveyed by Scripture. If we are only interested in "just the facts, please," we will have difficulty with much of the Bible. If, on the other hand, we are interested in what the Scripture means, then it opens endless resources and help and inspiration to us. That is its purpose.

The question of meaning is acute in us when we examine the gospel accounts of Jesus' birth. It is raised immediately by the star of Bethlehem: did that star really happen—just like that? If we are only interested in the answer to that question (even though we certainly may want to consider it), we will miss the story's real meaning.

It is meaning we need. Historical facts are important, but they are far from everything we need in life, especially in our faith. We may take a sentimental attitude toward facts, but by themselves facts do not help us move toward the heart of God. Ultimately, our desire for God is our motivation for approaching the manger. We seek Christ, who lives in our hearts and brings us to the fullness of divine love. This desire is not filled by facts alone. That Jesus came *then* can only matter to us if he also comes *now*, within us.

Our desire for Christ is filled only by Christ. He can, however, be deeply mediated to us through the meaning of Scripture *as we now have it,* when it is factual as well as when it is uncertain or not factual. For life-giving meanings, we must do two things. First, we must look into the Scripture as profoundly as we possibly can and include the insights of scholarship. And, second, we must open ourselves in prayer to experiencing God in Christ *through* Scripture, incorporating those same insights.

Incorporating means "embodying." When we try to live the Scripture, insights come. Then we put those insights into action: we pray with them, we include them in our decision making, we alter our behavior to resonate with them. If we continue, we grow gradually into living the full gospel. Since the Christmas stories are mini-gospels, we will look for ways to live them every day.

The purpose of this book is to help you find insights through *reading and thinking about* Scripture and to assist you to pray with what you learn. Suggestions will be made for enlivening Scripture within yourself by action. If you want to, you will be living the stories. Then, whether they are historical fact or inspired invention or older traditions of unknown origin—or all three—will not matter so much. Christmas will be alive in you. Jesus will have been born in your life, perhaps more deeply than ever before.

Gospels in Miniature

The stories around Jesus' birth are mini-gospels. They present the essence of the Good News of Jesus in story form. The stories are full of associations and hints—and we already know a great deal about them. The stories are full of reminders, especially about the Old Testament traditions. Since we may not be familiar with details from the Old Testament, these particular aspects of the stories may not be so clear to us. The stories are rich in symbols, too. These require pondering, and in pondering we are led to prayer and contemplation. As Luke says of Mary: she "kept all these things, reflecting on them in her heart" (Luke 2:19).

Since the Christmas stories are mini-gospels, we can expect that they are closely related to the gospels in which they appear. So first let's notice where they are. Some Christmas stories appear in Matthew and some in Luke. Mark says nothing at all about the birth of Jesus. John doesn't either; in place of stories, he has a glorious reflection on the meaning of the Incarnation. So we will examine the Gospels of Matthew and Luke for Christmas stories, then add a reflection on John's Prologue.

To Help Yourself

Many insights into scriptural meanings arise through comparison of texts. The Christmas stories need to be compared. Here is a suggestion to make your study easier:

Photocopy Matthew 1 and 2; Luke 1 and 2; Luke 3:23-38. Then cut away all footnotes. Cut the text into sections (usually a section is titled in bold type). Find the sections in Matthew that discuss the same topic or tell the same story as the sections in Luke. There will not be very many of these. Tape the sections beside one another on sheets of paper, so you can see at a glance which parts are found in both gospels and which parts are in only one of them. You may use the Appendix on pages 78 and 79 to help you sort them out quickly.

I also strongly recommended that you read this book with your Bible close by. You will want to read not only the Christmas stories but the Old Testament references that supplement them.

What Are the Facts?

Because of our twentieth-century interest in historical fact, scholars have researched exhaustively the details recounted in the gospel accounts of Jesus' infancy. Hundreds of pages have been published debating whether each incident in the Christmas stories actually happened as described. Some of the questions raised by scholars you probably have asked yourself, for example:

❋ If the star was so huge, why didn't everybody see it? Why are there no astronomical records of it?

❋ If angels filled the sky on the night of Jesus' birth, why did only the shepherds see them? Wouldn't everyone in Bethlehem have seen them?

❋ Did magi really come from the East? How many were there anyway? Why didn't the whole village of Bethlehem know the magi had been there?

❋ Why don't the genealogies of Jesus agree?

There are many similar questions. Most of them stem from two inescapable facts. The first is that, obviously, Matthew and Luke did not agree on very much. The second is that while historical information from other sources about the time of Jesus' birth is available, most of it either does not mention the events reported in the gospel account at all or it shows inaccuracies in the biblical stories. Let's consider these in order.

That Matthew and Luke agree on very little is obvious from a quick comparison of the two. The reason we may never have noticed the differences before is that in traditional Christmas customs, such as manger scenes, everything is amalgamated. Therefore, when we read Matthew, we know that the rest is there somewhere. When we read Luke, we likewise assume what we know from Matthew.

However, to see clearly the richness of these two mini-gospels, we must separate them and understand each one on its own terms. We will begin to do that in Chapter One.

As for the questions raised by other historical information, some scholars are primarily concerned with historical fact. Discussions, nuances, opinions, and "proofs" abound in their writings. Each scholar assesses things differently from others, and each prefers to emphasize different things. In this book, no attempt will be made to include and follow all such scholarly discussion.

In reality, the answer to many of our "Did it really happen?" questions is *"We do not know for sure."* The best Christian thinkers look at the evidence, sort it out, and draw their own conclusions. We cannot know exactly what happened, we cannot know exactly how the traditions were gathered, and we cannot know precisely how each writer and editor put together what is there.

Fact and Symbol

No matter how it happened, we want to get as much meaning as we can out of these wonderful stories so they can bring us closer to Christ. For that purpose, scholarship helps. Scholars thoroughly examine every letter of every passage and find things we would never find on our own. Christian biblical scholarship is a truly wonderful field.

We will also consider symbols in these stories. A symbol is anything—a form, such as a circle; something in nature, such as the sun; even a historical fact—that communicates higher truth to the reader. *A symbol is not merely something that stands for something else.* It is something available to our perception that imparts a higher truth. Symbols are real in their own right. The gospel writers included them for a purpose, and they are full of meaning. Look for them as you go through the Christmas stories.

Both Belong to Our Faith

Some facts are vital to our Christian faith. That Jesus really lived is vital! So are other events in his ministry, passion, and resurrection.

Other facts are not vital: a physical, traveling star—or the historical absence of such a star—will not affect our relationship with God. Whether or not the star is a historical fact, however, it is a symbol. It brings meaning to us in the context of the mini-gospel of Matthew, and that meaning enriches our understanding and supports our relationship to God.

Whether certain things *are* facts and symbols at the same time or symbols alone, we may not be able to determine. No doubt each of us will form an opinion about those items, but we will never know for sure. And that's all right. The meaning of those items will be available to us, and the meaning is the crux of the matter.

Both facts and symbols have a place in our growth in faith and in our spirituality—our relationship with God. That's why both will be included in our look at the Christmas stories.

So the writers of these mini-gospels gathered tradition, symbols, facts, and stories in order to evoke the truth within us. Our experience of that inner truth is the central interest of the gospels.

In the event of Jesus' birth, it became obvious that the spiritual and material worlds are not as distant from each other as we may imagine. All worlds come together in the Christmas stories: the extraordinary and the ordinary, the poor and the rich, the lowly and the exalted, the family and the angels—even nature plays its part in the form of a mysterious star. Together they evoke in us wonder at the reality of the Christ among us again—still.

Enchanted by the same wonder and seeking ways of expressing it, the writers of Matthew and Luke took the little historical detail they had and enriched it with allusions to the Old Testament—their Scripture and still ours today. They wanted to tell the whole truth of the birth of Jesus via such allusions. They wanted to evoke the heart's wonder at the mystery.

They were successful. Christians have refreshed their faith and enlivened their relationship to Christ through the Christmas stories for nearly two thousand years. We moderns, probably more than any previous people, need to have our sense of wonder at Jesus revitalized. Let's live with the Christmas stories more fully and give them an opportunity to do that.

Praying With Scripture

Before we begin our study of the Christmas stories, here is a suggestion for praying with them.

Praying the Scriptures *(lectio divina)* is a practice older than Christianity. The earliest Christians had only the Hebrew Bible (our Old Testament), but it is apparent they used it for understanding Jesus and for prayer. We can follow their example.

Praying with Scripture is not the same as studying it, nor is it a matter of "finishing the chapter." Praying with Scripture is a quiet, slow, open-hearted process in which we allow God to meet us through the words of the Bible. We cannot do this well if our minds are busily solving puzzles in the text. So when we come to Scripture for prayer, we are looking for a different approach.

Here is a simple beginning.

This is prayer. It aims first to put us in conscious contact with the Lord. We do it best alone and in a quiet place where we are not likely to be interrupted. Here in this special situation, we relax. We let our bodies and minds be quiet.

We turn first to the Lord, gratefully acknowledging his presence in us and in the words we are about to ponder. We offer this time to God for his action in us. We ask for divine blessings on our prayer.

Then we turn to the passage we have chosen and begin to read. Reading aloud is likely to slow us down a bit, which is desirable, as this reading is for savoring and for listening. With our attention attuned to our heart, we let our mind read along gently until something "strikes" us or seems to speak to us.

When that happens, we pause. We may repeat the significant word or phrase in our mind, letting it sink into our heart. We may even visualize it settling in our heart. We simply let the word be in us, and we remain attentive to it as long as it seems alive.

Sometimes insights come, sometimes not. Sometimes the truth of a phrase springs into vitality and opens new understanding. We may not even be able to put the newness into words, but we may experience it. Sometimes the whole experience is very still and contemplative. Then we may feel its beauty in the way we silently experience a sunset or gaze at a flower.

Whatever our experience, we stay with it as long as it communicates with us. Then, if we have time and wish to do so, we gently move along to more reading. We may repeat the process as often as we wish.

When our period of prayer is over, we close with thanksgiving for whatever has occurred. God will have been in the experience, whatever it was. God will give us in such prayer exactly what we need at that moment. So we thank the Lord for such attention and goodness to us.

This pattern of prayer with Scripture can be used with all the study of the Christmas stories. Other suggestions will be added as we go along, but please do not neglect the simple God-oriented savoring of the stories just as they are. They are the word of God to us.

CHAPTER ONE

The Writers
and Their Communities

Why do we have any infancy stories about Jesus? How did they come to be written?

As with most Scripture, more than one factor is involved. The most enlightening point is made by Father Raymond Brown in his classic study *The Birth of the Messiah*.

He reminds us that the Christian understanding of Jesus developed "backward," so to speak. As the first Christians pondered the meaning of their experience of Jesus, the Resurrection, and the coming of the Spirit into their hearts, they truly understood that Jesus was more than just a beloved teacher. They came to see that he was the Son of God.

At first, some thought that he "became" the Son of God at a particular time. It seemed natural to think that this moment was the Resurrection. The resurrected Jesus was the Son of

God, accepted into Sonship as he was raised from the dead by the Father.

As they continued to contemplate their experience and their faith, they realized that Jesus' characteristics during his ministry showed that he was the Son of God even then and not only at the time of Resurrection. So gradually that "moment" for becoming Son of God came to be placed at Jesus' baptism. Thus, Matthew 3:17 and Luke 3:38 announce that Jesus is the Son of God.

Then, Father Brown says, Christians began to believe that Jesus had been the Son of God from the first, that there had not been a moment in his lifetime when he "became" the Son of God.

Paul's letters support this picture of developing Christian reflection on Jesus. Paul's letters are the earliest Christian literature we have. They are filled with comments about Jesus crucified and risen, but they say nothing about either Jesus' baptism or birth.

Mark was the first of the gospels to be written, probably in the A.D. 60s. Mark says nothing about the birth of Jesus but begins with John the Baptist and Jesus' baptism. This indicates that the birth stories may not have been important to the Christians of that time. Mark does, however, announce that Jesus is the Son of God at his baptism.

Scholars generally agree that the gospels of Matthew and Luke were written at least twenty years later than Mark. Father Brown suggests that during this twenty-year period, Christian belief that Jesus was born the Son of God came to clear expression. Matthew and Luke reflect that belief by telling about the birth of Jesus to demonstrate that this baby was the Son of God.

Of course, neither the writer of Matthew nor of Luke can be imagined to have invented the stories out of nothing. They had some unwritten traditions about Jesus' infancy and early life that had probably circulated in the Christian communities. (Scholarship generally agrees, however, that these stories did not come from Mary, the Mother of Jesus. That is a devotional tradition that only shows up a good while after the writing of Matthew and Luke.)

These unwritten traditions seem to have included the birth of Jesus in Bethlehem, the raising of Jesus in Nazareth, the virginity of Mary at Jesus' birth, the conception of Jesus through the creative activity of the Holy Spirit, the "foster" fatherhood of Joseph, and the biological descent of Jesus from the lineage of King David. Both Matthew and Luke include all these important traditions, but the stories surrounding them are quite different in the two accounts.

There was also in the Christian community a keen awareness that Jesus the Christ fulfilled the predictions and analogies in their Scriptures—which were, of course, the Scriptures we call the Old Testament. So their reflection on the meaning of Jesus included searching the Old Testament for images, stories, or sections that could be understood as references to Jesus.

This was especially true for those Christians who were Jewish. At first, all Christians were Jewish. In a very short time, however, non-Jews (Gentiles) became Christians, too. Eventually, it was no longer possible to be both. The Jewish leaders did not allow it.

Gentiles, too, "inherited" the Jewish Scriptures, the Old Testament, and found there expressions of the meaning of Jesus. However, their feelings about the tradition would vary somewhat from that of their fellow Christians who were Jews.

Thus, a writer aiming primarily at a gentile audience would handle the Old Testament somewhat differently than one aiming at a mainly Jewish community. Since the gospel writers belonged to Christian communities themselves, they shared the growing understanding of all Christians. They searched the Old Testament for meanings relevant to Jesus that would communicate powerfully to their immediate communities.

If we seek to understand the infancy stories, therefore, we need to know something about the communities of Matthew and of Luke.

Matthew and His Community

Today's understanding of the gospels include the almost universal agreement that none of them were actually written down by an eyewitness. Indeed, only John claims a connection to an eyewitness, and even then the eyewitness seems to have been the bearer of the traditions, not the actual writer.

The Gospel of Matthew was most likely written around A.D. 85-90. It was written in good Greek, which is strong evidence that the writer was not one of the first disciples of Jesus, who were, after all, Galileans and Jews. Nevertheless, linguistic scholars tell us that certain elements of Aramaic style show up in the Greek, so the writer was probably bilingual and gathered his material from several sources (including Mark's Gospel).

But from A.D. 130, Christian writers *attributed* this gospel to Matthew, the tax collector who followed Jesus. Such an attribution raises major historical problems. (If you wish to examine this question further, look at a good commentary, such as *The Jerome Biblical Commentary.*)

The community of Matthew probably was in Syria, possibly Antioch, one of the strongest of the early communities. The Gospel of Matthew shows considerable knowledge of Jewish customs and laws but less awareness of Palestinian geography. So perhaps the writer of Matthew was a Jew who never lived in Palestine proper but in Syria.

In such a community, Jewish and gentile understandings of Christianity would have been in constant contact with each other, sometimes with more mutual understanding than at other times. The writer of Matthew's Gospel is interested in integrating these two forms of Christian understanding.

Since his community was predominately Jewish, Matthew emphasizes points that help them understand their Christian identity, including their community relationship to gentile Christians.

Although there is no direct evidence for it, scholars have often suggested that Matthew 13:52 might refer to the writer of the gospel: "Then every scribe who has been instructed in the kingdom of heaven is like the head of a household who brings from his storeroom both the new and the old." Was the writer of Matthew, then, a Jewish scribe who had become a Christian? It seems to fit—and that is the most that can be said.

Luke and His Community

No one has ever suggested that the Gospel of Luke was written by an eyewitness to Jesus and his ministry. It has, however, been universally recognized that the writer of Luke also wrote The Acts of the Apostles, so scholarly investigation of this writer's background has included both New Testament books.

For a long time, it was thought that the writer was the Luke who accompanied Paul on some of his missionary travels. More recent scholarship tends to the conclusion that this is not the case. There are notable exceptions, but in fact, we do not know for sure who wrote the Gospel of Luke.

Like the Gospel of Matthew, the Gospel of Luke was likely written no earlier than A.D. 85. The gospel shows confusion about Palestinian geography, so the writer probably never lived there. He wrote in excellent Greek—too good for a translation and reflecting considerable education. Greek was probably his mother tongue. He also knew the Greek Old Testament and employed some Greek literary techniques common to classical Greek composition. All this suggests that he was a Gentile from somewhere other than Palestine.

While Matthew cites the Old Testament often and directly, Luke uses allusions to known Jewish customs, values, and stories. This, combined with the strong emphasis on Paul in The Acts of the Apostles, suggests that Luke may have been a convert in the gentile mission. At any rate, he belonged to and wrote for a predominantly gentile community.

What was it like for a Gentile to step into a new faith that included a long tradition? We can only surmise. The gentile's experience of Jesus would be interior, not physical, so it might seem desirable to get some grounding in a history related to Jesus. The Gentile would want some assurance that he or she belonged to the Old Testament tradition, too. Many wanted to learn about the Old Testament and spent the rest of their lifetime studying it. Others—like many of us—were not content to know what Christianity meant to them as it was.

But all new gentile Christians must have wanted assurance that Jesus did not just appear in a vacuum but that God *intended* both Jesus and Christianity all along. Gentiles might not have been so interested in specific verses of Jewish Scripture, but they would have wanted to see connections. That conviction and hope sent them to the Scriptures, the Old Testament, and there they found what they sought.

Christians in the A.D. 80s

Both Matthew and Luke, then, were written in the A.D. 80s. What was it like to be a Christian in that decade?

First, we may notice that living connections to the Jewish background of Christianity had been greatly weakened by this time. In part, this was caused by changes within the Jewish community itself. In A.D. 70 Rome, having finally lost patience with repeated armed uprisings in Palestine, had crushed the Jewish resistance, this time destroying the center of Jewish identity. The Temple in Jerusalem was no more.

Therefore, the Jewish community in the A.D. 80s was struggling for survival. Because of that, opposition to Jews who were Christians—and to Christianity in general—was greatly increased. The fact that Jews and Christians used the same Scriptures only made matters worse, for each group felt that the interpretations made by the other were either misguided or incomplete.

Yet the question of the relation of Christianity to the Jewish tradition was, as we have just seen, not just a Jewish question. Gentile Christians cared about it, too. How these two groups of Christians could live together and share their faith continued to be an issue.

In a given local community, there might be only Jewish Christians or only gentile Christians, but in most communities—and certainly in Matthew's—there were both. They had to learn from each other what it meant to be more Christian than either Jewish or Gentile. It could not have been easy.

One influence that kept all Christians close, however, was the possibility of persecution. Arrest and torture of Christians as such was not official Roman policy until the late A.D. 90s. Nevertheless, Christians had suffered for their faith long before that.

Inhabitants of the Roman Empire were required to pay at least nominal homage to Roman gods unless they were Jews. Judaism was a legal Roman religion. For a long time, Christianity was included in Judaism under Roman law, since Rome was not interested in sectarian differences among Jews. After the destruction of the Temple, however, Judaism began to repudiate Christianity openly. Moreover, the growing number of Gentiles in Christian communities made it less and less possible for Christians to claim the legal status of Judaism.

The situation was ambiguous in the A.D. 80s, but Luke does show a desire to enhance Christian status in the eyes of Roman law.

By that time, almost no one who remembered Jesus firsthand was still living. This was one reason why the traditions and practices of Jesus' earliest followers began to be recorded.

By this time, too (fifty years after Jesus had departed his physical life), Christians began to think that the Church might have a longer earthly existence than they had originally anticipated. The importance of recording the truth, of Church organization, of how to teach and live in this open-ended period, all became more urgent. Gospels (among other writings) were composed from traditions (including Mark), from current understandings, and from the Old Testament.

All these factors probably figured in the writing of the infancy stories about Jesus.

The Infancy Stories and Our Spiritual Growth

It is almost impossible for us to imagine what our Christian year would be like if we had no Christmas stories. We simply take them for granted as part of our Christian life and faith.

Since they are mini-gospels and aim to proclaim Jesus Christ, they give us a good deal of information about Jesus, most of it quite familiar. Of course, we can always take that information to a deeper level of understanding. Perhaps our most immediate interest, however, is what the infancy stories mean to us spiritually. Do they make any contribution to our spirituality? Do they *help* us grow spiritually?

Yes, they do. Or they can—if we open ourselves to their wonderful influence.

These stories actively evoke within us qualities and characteristics necessary to continued spiritual growth. The very fact that they are stories invite us to hear them with our whole selves and not only as sources of information. Whose heart does not perk up at the words "once upon a time"? These stories invite that alertness.

When this happens, our awareness is expanded. As we learn about the symbols and associations, each word, each phrase, is filled up for us, evoking more and more in our awareness. Every bit of expanded awareness tends toward our spirit. The wider of heart we are, the keener our consciousness, the more receptive we are to God. Further, by pondering the characters in these stories, our hearts can be opened.

When I was considering becoming a Catholic, an old priest, Father Leo Kulleck, C.SS.R., began to talk to me. In the framework of the mysteries of the rosary and the Seven Dolors rosary, he told me enlarged versions of the Christmas story. He had spent a lifetime living with these stories and their possibilities, his heart full of devotion. In his retelling, the characters in the stories came newly alive: Mary, Joseph, the baby, and all the others who appear in these stories—and some who don't!

At some point in his telling, I ceased to care whether the stories were historically true or if everything he said could actually be found in the Bible. Instead of a desire for precise information, I found myself using the characters as symbols of their choices, their difficulties, and their willingness to undertake big challenges.

The stories evoked love in my heart. In those moments, facts did not matter. Love mattered. And what is love? It is God. It is the basis and goal of every spiritual intention, every spiritual effort. This is a key to living and praying the infancy stories.

Once a woman told a priest that she was worried because she felt no love for God. He regarded her gently, then asked if she loved anyone. Her face softened. "Oh, yes," she said. "I love my baby son very much."

"Then," replied the wise priest, "can you love the baby Jesus, Mary's son?" Of course, she could. And she could love Mary, too, because she had experienced young motherhood. In loving the baby Jesus, she soon found that her capacity to love had grown and God was no longer an abstraction for her.

Every part of the Christmas stories has a similar potential: the possibility of unlocking us to love. If we want this to happen, we can offer ourselves attentively to the Christmas stories at every level. The more information we have, the more powerful may be our whole-person response, for we should never try to leave behind our reasoning mind. The more associations and symbols we include in our study, the broader and deeper will be our personal understanding of all God's wonderful design for life.

In *How to Read and Pray the Christmas Story,* we seek information, we explore associations and symbols, and we open our hearts to the characters in the stories, ready to examine them and enlarge them. We also seek the writers' intentions. Then we turn to action—ways of living the stories in our own daily lives.

CHAPTER TWO

The Christmas Story in Matthew

Before we begin a discussion of Matthew's story of the birth of Jesus, it will help you to read it. It is found in the first two chapters of the gospel. Even if you have read it recently, open your Bible now and read through Matthew 1 and 2 several times. Read with a notepad and pencil or pen at hand, and if questions arise, jot them down to consider later.

The Genealogy of Jesus
Matthew 1:1-17 and Luke 3:23-38

The Gospel of Matthew begins with a genealogy of Jesus. Luke's Gospel places this genealogy after Jesus' baptism. These verses are not our favorite kind of reading and must throw homilists into near panic. Yet they offer both information and the beginning of reflection.

Take a few moments to read both genealogies. Then read them a second time, comparing the two as you go. Notice the differences between the first and last verses of each. Can you tell who is the most important ancestor in each list? Can you discern the main point of each list?

Each genealogy has a definite purpose. From the standpoint of historical fact alone, it is impossible to reconcile the differences in the two lists—though the attempts have been ingenious.

Amid the differences, a striking commonality is that Abraham and David are included in both lists. (If you do not recall much about these men, you may review them in Genesis 11:27–23:20 and 1 Samuel 16–31, 2 Samuel, and 1 Kings 1–2.)

Matthew's list begins Jesus' lineage with Abraham. In Jewish tradition, Abraham was the first to be in covenant with the Lord God. He was the ancestor of all Jews, the receiver of God's promises, and a man of profound and obedient faith. For Christians, Abraham is a supreme example of the beauty and power of trustful obedience to God.

Moreover, Christians believe that a new covenant was established by Jesus that fulfilled, but by no means ended, previous covenants of the Old Testament. The early Christians experienced themselves as a new people. Moreover, they saw in Jesus a perfect example of total trust and total obedience to the Father. So they revered Abraham, too.

Jesus' descent from King David is part of the tradition of the Messiah. The Messiah was expected to be a king like David, being his distant "son," and to unify the Jewish people again into an independent nation. In Matthew, the ancestors named from David to Jechoniah are kings of Israel.

Christians accepted this tradition but redefined it to fit their experience of Jesus. Jesus' first disciples saw him potentially in a political role, but experience showed that in Jesus "messiah-ship" was aimed not at politics but at eternity. *Messiah* means "anointed one," and Jesus' followers experienced him as profoundly anointed by God, but for spiritual purposes, not political ones.

Four women are mentioned in Jesus' ancestry, all in Matthew's list.

❋ Tamar (Genesis 38) was being slighted by her father-in-law, so she tricked him into having sexual intercourse with her and bore a son as a result.

❋ Rahab (Joshua 2 and 6) was a prostitute who helped Joshua spy on Jericho so he could conquer it later.

❋ Ruth (Book of Ruth) was a Moabite who came to Israel out of loving loyalty to her mother-in-law; she became David's great-grandmother.

❋ Bathsheba (called Solomon's mother in the list; see 2 Samuel 11 and 12, 1 Kings 1) was the woman with whom King David committed adultery. He then arranged that her husband be killed in battle so he could marry her.

Why *these* four women in Jesus' genealogy? Others might have been included but weren't. Scholars generally conclude that there is an irregularity about the birth of each woman's son. This irregularity prepares the knowledgeable reader for the "irregularity" of Jesus' birth: Mary's virginity.

For the writer of Matthew, the genealogy connects Jesus firmly with the Old Testament as a flowering of the messianic tradition. It affirms that Jesus was the Messiah who was always intended in the divine design for Israel.

In Luke, the genealogy follows Jesus' baptism, at which time Jesus is announced as Son of God (Luke 3:22). Luke's list then shows how this divine descent occurred in human terms. It traces Jesus' ancestry to Adam and then to God.

But we today know already that Jesus is Messiah and Son of God. So what is there in the genealogies for us?

Living the Genealogies

The writers of the genealogies placed Jesus in honorable lineages but hardly superhuman ones (except, of course, for God in Luke). The life stories of each of the known characters in these lists are lives of a quality like ours. While they were notable in history, some were good people, some not so good, and some were good people with serious weaknesses. They struggled in their faith and their lives. None had it any easier than we do, and they made just as many mistakes—some of them dramatic!

Yet Jesus "came from" them. He came right into the midst of human life with all its mixed qualities. Although later Christians believed that God chose a special person to be Jesus' mother, all the rest were pretty ordinary humans. The lists put Jesus in a totally human context.

That can be quite comforting. Often we are so acutely aware of our failings and inadequacies that we forget that Jesus can be born in our midst as well. That is why Jesus came through ordinary people: to assure us that we, too, can know God through him, right in our everyday life. He came to human beings, as a human being, *for* human beings.

Of the women in Matthew's list, only one (Ruth) is wholly admirable. (The men aren't so wholly admirable, either!) The presence of these women says something wonderful: no matter how skewed our lives get, God's design for great goodness goes on. It goes on in spite of our wrongs and confusions. It even uses our weaknesses sometimes. God's design for human well-being, for our salvation into his abundant life, marches forward regardless of our sometime idiocies.

Knowing the stupid things I have done, I can only be profoundly grateful for God's powerful faithfulness to goodness. We can rely on God's faithfulness to his design for goodness, no matter how many awful things seem to go on in us or around us.

If we choose to cooperate with God's marvelous design, then we get to enjoy it and find intense fulfillment in it. If we don't so choose, it goes on anyway (only *we* may miss out on its joys). That certainly provides a steady center for our life on earth.

Let's take the time to meditate long and attentively on God's steady design for goodness. Let the sense of it seep deeply into our being.

❋ ❋ ❋ ❋ ❋ ❋

Next time the gospel reading at Mass is a genealogy, instead of thinking how endless this list of unknown names is, let's recall a deeper message: these are people like us, and Jesus, Messiah, and Son was willing to be born from them. Let's say "Alleluia!"

The Birth of Jesus
Matthew 1:18-25

First, reread this section so it is fresh. Notice that nothing is said here about the location of either Joseph's home or Jesus' birth. That comes in Matthew 2:1.

Matthew says that Jesus was born of a virgin named Mary. He certainly wants us to know that Jesus is "Son of David" and "Son of God" as well. Yet the emphasis here is not on Mary. Mary is mentioned by name only twice in Matthew's birth stories (1:18 and 2:11). The main character is Joseph.

Through Joseph, Matthew makes more connections with the Old Testament. The dream of Joseph is reminiscent of the other Joseph who dreamed true dreams: the son of Jacob and ruler of Egypt (Genesis 37–50).

The key theme shared by both Josephs is saving acts of God through people. Through the first Joseph, God saved the family of Israel (Jacob) from famine. Now, God worked through another Joseph to bring salvation in Jesus. A Jew of the time, versed in his own tradition, would see the parallel right away. Matthew also stresses God's fulfillment of his ancient design by citing specific Old Testament passages.

What does *fulfillment* mean? Often we think of it as a specific prediction that "came true." Throughout Christian tradition, however, many have seen fulfillment more as an Old Testament archetype made real and full in the life of Jesus. The writer of Matthew expresses this fuller sense. For him, the *meanings* (both factual and symbolic) of the Old Testament were opened, completed, made full in Jesus Christ. The "old" era has expanded to include newness and to become full of new qualities, that is, fulfilled.

Fulfillment of the Prophet

To understand the story of the birth, we need to know about two Jewish customs: betrothal and the naming of a baby.

In Palestine at the time, betrothal was as serious as marriage. The two young people (often thirteen or fourteen years old) were promised to each other, but the young woman remained in the home of her parents for a period of time. During that time the young man visited the family, and the two became better acquainted. The actual marriage was simply the young woman's move to the home of her husband's family.

Scholars disagree about whether the couple would have

sexual intercourse during betrothal. Matthew indicates clearly that Mary and Joseph did not, since Joseph knew Mary's child was not his. He thought she had committed adultery against her promise to him. Had this been proven true, he could legally have had her stoned to death.

Even though Joseph lived according to the Law—that's what *righteous* means—he didn't want to have Mary stoned. He was simply going to divorce her without public notice.

Thanks to the divine message, however, Joseph came to understand about Mary's child, and in 1:25 we read that "he named him Jesus." According to the Jewish law, this act of naming the baby publicly announced his own legal paternity. Jewish law had long before recognized that paternity is often difficult to determine, so the culture had come to value *legal* paternity above biological paternity.

This is different from our modern view, indeed. But it meant that Jesus could have a father and a mother, even though he was conceived "through the Holy Spirit" and born of a virgin.

Matthew cites the Book of Isaiah in 1:23, saying that Jesus' birth fulfilled this prophecy. It's a little difficult to see that, for the situation in Isaiah is totally different. Moreover, Jesus is not named Emmanuel at his birth.

As indicated in this instance, Matthew's Old Testament citations about fulfillment do not always seem to fit very well. That is not really the point, however. The point is the reiteration that God had planned for Jesus all through Israel's history.

Can We Live Like Joseph?

Without Joseph, almost nothing in Matthew's birth story would have been possible. It would have turned out wrong. Joseph is the mainstay of this sacred moment in history, the birth of our Lord. Let's consider Joseph.

First, he is faced with a terrible choice: what to do with his new wife, whom he seriously suspects of adultery. We are told nothing of his struggle, but it must have been agony. Had he been inclined to revenge, he had every legal right to it.

Before his dream, Joseph decides that he will not treat Mary according to the full possibility of the Law but be compassionate to her and simply dissolve their betrothal.

Notice that God does not give Joseph any helpful information until this compassionate decision is made. God often lets us struggle with our agonies long enough to grow from them and to make our own decision. Only then does the Lord (sometimes) give us specific and unmistakable help or direction.

Joseph was already righteous, obedient to the Law. In his agonizing decision, Joseph won through to a higher kind of righteousness, the righteousness of compassion. He did not flout the Law but was ready to use it compassionately.

Maybe only the compassionate heart is open enough to receive God's guidance clearly. Notice what God's messenger gives Joseph: reassurance that Mary has not committed adultery (1:20) and that the Holy Spirit has created something new in her. Joseph is directed to take Mary home and to name the child (1:21, legal paternity). The name indicates the mission of Jesus: to "save his people from their sins" (1:21).

Compassion has opened Joseph to hear the Lord's word. His own decision is reversed by the Lord. Then Joseph simply obeys (1:24).

Have you ever wished God would decide *for* you? Or at least that you could count on his correction if you have decided wrongly?

Sometimes such a wish is simply a refusal of responsibility

or a fear that a wrong decision is irrevocable and could be destructive. Other times our wish for God to tell us how to decide is a deep desire to know God's will and a readiness to obey.

Joseph instructs us here, perhaps, about how to receive God's guidance. He is already living up to the best he knows; he is "righteous." He goes through whatever he must as circumstances meet him. He is not afraid to decide and decides on the basis of compassion. Do we do as well?

To help yourself live as Joseph did, you may wish to ask yourself the following questions as prelude to prayer.

* Do I obey quickly and easily when I have received God's guidance?
* Do I act on what I already know?
* If I ignore guidance, what can I expect from God the next time I need help?
* When praying for guidance, do I first do everything in my own power toward reaching a decision?
* What is my own attitude toward rules? Is keeping the rules as important—or more important—to me as acting in love?
* What is the highest criterion I usually use for making decisions?

Now let your body and reflective mind slow down, relax, become quiet. Gently turn your attention to God within your own being. Turn your self-insights into prayer in the form most comfortable for you.

※ ※ ※ ※ ※ ※

The Magi
Matthew 2:1-12

Who are these magi? This is the only time they are mentioned anywhere in the Bible.

The words *magus* (singular) and *magi* (plural) appear in other writings, however. There they seem to be priests in ancient Persia who had considerable education and some unusual powers. Some magi could interpret dreams and visions, others studied the heavens and drew knowledge from the night sky, some seemed to know deep secrets of wisdom. They were often wealthy because in their own society their status was high.

In Matthew, the term *magi* is not explained. The writer assumed that his readers would understand. Matthew does not say exactly where they came from, only "the east" (2:1). At the very least, these magi are observers of the sky, astronomer/astrologers, respected in the culture. One thing is clear: these Gentiles—intelligent, well-placed ones—recognized the Lord from the very beginning. Even though they did not have the help of the Hebrew Scriptures, God communicated with them through nature (the stars). Gentiles, too, could rejoice and pay homage to the newborn Jesus.

Then they exit, never to reappear.

Was this visit historical, factual? There are problems with the whole scene. For one thing, King Herod did not have the power to call together the chief priests and scribes (2:4). Jewish leaders were at odds with Herod and would not have been so available. Furthermore, Bethlehem was a village. Such exotic visitors would have caused an everlasting memory. Surely, Mary and Joseph would have been known, for in Matthew, Bethlehem is apparently assumed to be Joseph's hometown (1:20, 24). (Notice that there is no cave or stable in Matthew.)

Of course, the moving star leading the way from Jerusalem to Bethlehem and indicating the right house (2:9-11) is questionable. No astronomical phenomenon qualifies for this, even though astronomers have tried for centuries to find a star or comet or planetary conjunction that matched these conditions.

Most scholars conclude that this visit of the magi is unlikely to have happened. It cannot be proved either way.

What Can the Magi Teach Us?

Fact or not, the magi are in the Scriptures and loved in our tradition. What are the meanings in the magi that we may take into our hearts and ponder?

Once again, we are asked by Matthew to consider the design of God. Just as Jesus came as a Jew, so the Gentiles were informed and invited right from the start. That's good for us, too, as gentile Christians.

If these splendid visitors are viewed as symbolic, we see that they are definitely not poor and lowly in any economic or educational sense. They are rich, judging from the gifts they bring (2:11). They are highly educated and bear high status in their own country. So sure were they of their social position that they sought Jesus in the king's palace in Jerusalem.

But before the newborn Jesus they "prostrated themselves" (2:11). The magnificent of the world here make themselves lowly before a baby. Why? Because they know this baby has a magnificent purpose and destiny. Even the rich and the wise bow before him.

If the wise and the splendid acknowledge Jesus, what about our ordinary selves?

The gifts the magi bring have associations with the Old Testament, especially Isaiah 60:6. Isaiah was a favorite book of early Christians because they found in it so much they could refer to Jesus. Moreover, the gifts have symbolic value. Gold is the "highest" of metals, the most valuable, full of light, the best in its own (mineral) world. Incense is only offered in worship to God and not used for anything else, so it is the highest sacrifice. Myrrh is a fragrant resin often used in embalming a corpse. Each gift-symbol applies fittingly to Jesus. The highest value, the highest worship—yet death still must come.

Living With the Magi

We see in the story of the magi and Herod two tendencies in human beings. The magi are willing to journey far, bringing gifts of homage and valuables to the Lord. Herod wants to know about the new "ruler" only to destroy him. Both tendencies exist in us, though maybe not in such extreme form.

We have the capacity to say yes to God, to go on a long interior journey to experience the presence of Jesus in our heart. We, too, have been offered a "star"—the great possibility of new life in Christ. This possibility *is* historical! It's for now and here. The question is, do we set out? Are we willing to make the inward trek, not knowing exactly how it will turn out? The magi journeyed, perhaps, based on a long devotion to inner wisdom and deep knowledge of nature. We have revelation, tradition, Scripture. Do we go?

We also have the capacity to destroy, in and for our own selves, this newborn Jesus. It's a horrible thought, but we do have mighty resistances inside us. We don't like to face them. Of course, we would not destroy Jesus externally, physically. But in our heart or the hearts of others, do we sometimes destroy or want to destroy the presence of love? Do we ever flee the truth?

Let us pray that, like the magi, we will be able to do full

homage to the Lord within our being. Let's pray to be able to honor the Lord without reservations.

On seeing only a star, the magi set out on a long, uncomfortable, and expensive journey. They did not know for sure where they would find what they sought, nor when. But they went. They saw the star, perhaps, only because they were in the habit of observing the heavens.

They teach us, first, to keep our eyes open in the direction of what we believe. So often we tend to take our faith for granted, not watching over it or protecting it or trying to stretch it. If a new star appeared in that aspect of our life, the area of faith, would we notice it? So if we want to live out the magi story, we start looking for hints, for visions, for directions and pointers to experiencing and loving the King of our lives.

Then, when we are blessed with a star (a hint, a vision), the magi say to us, "Get going!" To follow a star both requires and develops wonderful qualities. Given the likely terrain of the magi's journey, it was challenging for them. The qualities I imagine in their journey, besides sheer stamina, are courage to move forward happily into the unknown. They needed insight: to see the star, to proceed on the journey, to know the next step, the next turn. If such qualities were not strong at the beginning of their trek, they must have been strong at its ending.

The magi teach us, too, to rejoice. When they received the guidance of the star, they rejoiced. People who have a great vision (like union with God) are guided again and again to their next steps. If they get sidetracked, going off to see some Herod, their vision itself will guide them onto the right path again. Indeed, that is cause for rejoicing—that the right direction has been found again and that trust in God is again rewarded by guidance.

Then the magi offer gifts to him. We do not carry quantities of gold or incense or myrrh. What inner gifts could we offer that might correspond to the symbols of the magi's gift? What do we value highest of all? That could be our gold. What, then, could be our incense? Perhaps a constant flow of worship and praise to the Lord from our heart. And myrrh for him? We can honor his death, keep it always close to our awareness, with reverence and thanksgiving.

Notice that after having worshiped the infant Jesus, the magi went home "another way." Another route may have been the surface meaning, but isn't something more suggested here? Doesn't a genuine open encounter with Jesus always change something inside us? Then we are enabled to live "another way." In Christian growth, we do not retrace our steps. We are moved always forward, toward the total transformation that the Lord invites us to experience.

Suggestions for Prayer and Reflection

Here is an experiment you may wish to try.

The next time you get a blazingly attractive idea, instead of tossing it away on the grounds of lack of money or some other variable, PAUSE. Ask God in your own heart if it might really be a good idea after all. Is it a star for you? Take it to prayer. Pray it through. Before you decide whether or not to follow this particular star, be determined to ignore hesitations like these: a sense of inadequacy, fears, the inability to see exactly how it will go.

If you find the idea to be good one, worthy and beautiful, chart your course, buy your camel, and go! Pray all the way.

For your reflection:

✳ When did I miss a valuable opportunity because I did not follow my star?

✳ Is there a star for my whole life? If not, do I want one? (You can always ask the Lord for one.) If so, how consistently do I follow it?

✼ Have I a vision that keeps me moving forward toward the Lord's full birth in me? What do I do that is my own journey toward him?

✼ Is my journey joyful? Do I rejoice at every bit of guidance coming my way?

For prayer, choose a time that is pretty open-ended. Settle into quiet for *lectio divina.* (Review, if necessary, Praying With Scripture, page 14.) Read slowly until a phrase or a connection jumps out at you. Let it sink deep down into your very body. If you want to put more words around it, as a verbal prayer to the Lord, do it. Perhaps the depth will leave you in silence. If so, rest there for as long as you can.

✼ ✼ ✼ ✼ ✼ ✼

The Flight to Egypt
Matthew 2:13-15

This little piece of the Christmas tradition is not found in Luke or anywhere else. It fits Matthew's intention.

Joseph has another dream. He obeys. The family heads for Egypt.

Egypt was the traditional place of refuge for people in trouble in Palestine. Throughout Old Testament history, prophets and kings and lesser people fled to Egypt to save their lives. Joseph (in Genesis) and his family were not the first, but they were the most important. That time, the Israelites stayed in Egypt for five hundred years. While there, the Hebrews became conscious of themselves as a people.

Matthew points out once again that this act of Joseph's

fulfilled the Scriptures. The prophet Hosea (11:1) says, "Out of Egypt I called my son." Hosea lived about 750 B.C. He was looking back to the Hebrew people, the figurative "son" of Yahweh, who were delivered out of Egypt under Moses' leadership. But early Christians saw in Jesus the true Son of God and so took the prophecy to heart. Joseph and Mary in Egypt parallel that ancient journey.

Our Own Flight to Egypt

As Matthew tells it, the message from the Lord and Joseph's immediate obedience provide protection for Mary and Jesus. They go to a place long used as a refuge. Is there such a place for us?

Yes, there is, but it may be a longer and harder journey than the one from Palestine to Egypt. Or it may be quicker if we are wholehearted! That place of refuge is the heart of God. Psalms speak often of it. In Psalms 2:11, we read "Happy are all who take refuge in God!" And in Psalms 7:2 the poet, beset by danger, writes "LORD, my God, in you I take refuge; rescue me; save me."

When we feel endangered by troubles, whether from the inside or from outer circumstances, when we are aware of great need, we can take refuge in the Lord.

What does that mean?

It means turn to God and *pray* with all your heart. It means throw yourself before the Lord with dependence on no other, willing to stay there. It means trusting that the Lord can and will protect you from *real* danger, those inner enemies that destroy our peace and keep us from full union with God. It means that the Lord will do much more for you than you imagine when you take total, continual refuge in him.

Taking refuge also means willingness to obey directions.

Joseph would hardly have been protected if he said, "I take refuge in the Lord, so I don't need to go to Egypt!" When we have turned our causes over to God, we may well be given guidance. If we want the effects planned by God for us, we want to follow that guidance, just as surely as Joseph obeyed the angels and the magi followed the star. We may not be allowed to "sit at home" and have every safety and help come walking in our door. We may have to act. In our obedience, we will experience God's protection.

What inner struggles are currently vivid in you? Go to God as your refuge, asking for help and deliverance. Turn all your insight into prayer for understanding and freedom.

The Massacre of the Infants
Matthew 2:16-18

It's a terrible thought, this massacre of babies—and it probably did not happen. Scholars think it is not historical because the Jewish historian Josephus, who hated Herod, does not include it in his list of Herodian atrocities (even though it would not have been out of character for this king). Moreover, traditions having to do with Bethlehem mention no such event. Such a horror would surely have been remembered outside Christian circles.

Again, Matthew's purpose in including this incident is to make connections with the Old Testament, specifically with the deliverance from Egypt. In Exodus 1:15-22, we read that the Hebrews lived under a policy that called for extermination of their male children, even though they were often able to evade it. Then later, when Moses was persuading the Pharaoh to let the Hebrews leave, an angel of death came and smote the firstborn son of all Egypt but passed over the Hebrew families (Exodus 11:1–12:36).

Thus, the first Passover was observed. Matthew may be pointing back to that tradition as well as forward to Jesus' last Passover before the passion, when this "Son out of Egypt" will be killed for the deliverance of all peoples.

Once again, Matthew's Jesus is shown recapitulating and enriching the life of Israel, even through the events surrounding his birth.

The story of the massacre of the innocents contrasts starkly with the story of the magi's visit. The magi pay homage to Jesus; Herod destroys many children in his attempt to destroy Jesus. In showing us two widely different responses to Jesus, Matthew seems to intend that very contrast. Equivalent differences show up throughout the gospel: some love, honor, and follow Jesus; others plot—and successfully—to have him killed.

We said in the Introduction that the birth stories are mini-gospels. Nowhere is that clearer than in these sharply contrasting incidents in Matthew's Gospel. Jesus is good news, but some love him and some hate him.

Living the Story

This is a tough one, isn't it? What in this horrible story of the destruction of innocent babies could have to do with our own lives?

Perhaps we could look closely at our destructive tendencies. Some may seem small. What about lashing out in anger when we are threatened (which is, after all, what Herod was doing)? When do we, with our tongues or even our thoughts, try to destroy someone else's influence or position or potential in order to promote ourselves? Do we try to create fear in other people? If we encounter one who is innocent or naive, do we try to change that quality? There are myriad ways in which humans attack one another. Some of them are very subtle. Some are so habitual, they are almost invisible to us.

It may be all too easy for us to assume that only other people have destructive tendencies or that only others indulge them. Yet until selfishness is eradicated from our heart, until our soul stands before God without egocentric interests, we are likely to be capable of some form of destruction. If it scares us to think of ourselves in that way, well—it should. Yet if such tendencies are there, it is vital that we face them. Only then can we take any action to soften them. Only then can we beg God to remove them from us.

Living this story may mean simply being willing to mourn over our own destructive capabilities as Rachel mourned over her children. Such mourning as that will bear good fruit.

Is rejecting Jesus inwardly as devastating to us, to our spiritual potential, as Herod's destruction of infants' lives? Why do you think so? Have you experienced this in your own life?

If you have reflected on your destructive tendencies, take your findings into your prayer. Ask the Lord to show you what you most need to see, to guide you in making necessary changes, and to do for you whatever you are unable to do for yourself.

When you have laid before the Lord all the difficulties you can presently see, try this brief visualization. Imagine Jesus watching you enact your heaviest destructive tendency. In your mind, do it all right before him; do it so that both of you may see it clearly.

Then, when it is exhausted, pause. Look into Jesus' face to find there *total compassion.* With your attention fixed on the love in his eyes, ask him to remove this tendency so that you may never be a Herod to anything innocent and beautiful in the Lord's world.

This prayer is *never* ignored. Be poised for new freedom!

The Return From Egypt
Matthew 2:19-23

This scene is the sequel to the Flight into Egypt. Again, the Lord sends an angelic messenger to direct Joseph. Again, Joseph obeys.

Here we find a reference to Moses and Exodus. Moses had killed someone, so he fled from Egypt to save his life (Exodus 2:15). But eventually the Lord commanded him to return to Egypt, since "all the men who sought your life are dead" (Exodus 4:19). Jesus, this allusion suggests, not only reenacts the life of Israel but is a "new" Moses as well. Who was Moses? The deliverer of Israel and the prototype of Jesus' spiritual mission.

It is generally reckoned that the family may have been in Egypt about two years. From what is known of the history of the time, it would seem that Jesus was born about 6 B.C. by modern calculations. King Herod died in 4 B.C., and his kingdom was divided among his three sons. Of these, Archelaus ruled Judea. He was cruel, so Joseph had reason to be uneasy, even without another dream.

Joseph took his family to Galilee, ruled by Herod Antipas, which was more peaceful and secure. Matthew suggests that security motivated Joseph's decision.

Looking at the composition, though, we see that the writer of Matthew had a problem to solve. He had two separate traditions: that Jesus was born in Bethlehem and that he grew up in (came from) Nazareth in Galilee. The Gospel of Luke has the same traditions, but he handles them differently.

Matthew makes Bethlehem Joseph and Mary's original home, but it was unfit for raising Jesus because it was dangerous. So after returning from Egypt, they go to Galilee to live.

Luke does something different. He posits that Joseph and Mary had their original home in Nazareth and were visiting Bethlehem at the time of the birth. But in Luke there is nothing about Egypt, because Luke's interests are different. Again, historical accuracy escapes us.

Joseph and Egypt—and Us

If Jesus is the new deliverer of Israel, as Matthew wants his readers to conclude, then we, who were never held captive in a physical Egypt, have to turn inward to understand the story's relationship to us.

What is our inner captivity?

We have an awareness of ourselves as individuals, but our individuality feels separate from everything, everyone. Many of us feel trapped by our personalities, our bodies, our past, our imagined future. We try to do good, to be good, to fill our lives with love. But we do not find it easy or sometimes even possible. You will know your personal captivities better than anyone; it sometimes helps to name them. Egypt symbolizes all these personal captivities.

It is easy to say quickly that deliverance ultimately is "from sin." But even though we say that, so far sinfulness continues to plague most of us at some level or other. How are we to understand this? Deliverance can best be understood by considering it at two levels, the universal and the personal.

Simply put, Jesus' deliverance of humanity on the universal level freed us from *inevitable* bondage to a life of separation from God and therefore in sinfulness. This salvation has been explained in many ways over the centuries. For us at this season, however, it may be enough to recognize that Jesus was born in order to accomplish this deliverance from inevitable captivity to our selfishness. He enabled people to be reconciled—brought back to the Father—and to live in full oneness with God.

We might think of it as opening a door before us that had been locked. However, there is no guarantee that this great act of deliverance will be appropriated by any particular individual. Many never choose to go through that door. For Jesus' universal work to be effective for a given person, that person must assimilate Jesus into his or her own life—or, rather, must allow Jesus to assimilate him or her into the divine life. That is the personal level of deliverance. It is the level of Jesus' work that can become true in our own experience.

It is glorious to glimpse the universal dimensions of Jesus' mission. But if he is not an active force in our own daily living, we are in fact still in captivity.

We may use Joseph as an analogy for our reflection.

Jesus is born into the world. Joseph acknowledges that, experiences it. Joseph *claims* the baby Jesus, names him, takes him to himself. Having done this, Joseph obeys any instructions he receives from God in regard to Jesus. We can claim Jesus, too, by acknowledging that he came for us, that he belongs to us (not exclusively but truly), and that we belong to him. If we do that, obedience comes as a natural response.

Some people are helped in this by thinking specifically of the baby Jesus. If I take the baby into my care, then I want to do what is good for the baby's growth just as Joseph did. What is good for Jesus' growth within us? Obedience to his adult teachings, for he gave us plenty of instruction!

Even in captivity, Joseph is with Jesus, for Jesus has entered his life and has gone to Egypt with him. Together they also leave Egypt, and Joseph is delivered just as all Israel was once delivered.

For us, too, Jesus is born. That much is world history. We

live in a kind of Egypt inside ourselves. Jesus enters that inner Egypt in order to bring us out of it into a full and peaceful life where we know and love Jesus and know and love God. It is a kind of inner "promised land."

This promised land is not a place but a condition. It is a deepening relationship with the Lord, to culminate, if we desire it, in full union with God. Union is deliverance out of every limitation and sin of our human nature to full interior freedom in love. If Jesus came to open such a door to all, he came also to encourage us to step through it and follow him to God. To accept this possibility for ourselves, we have to claim Jesus and obey him.

Suggestions for Prayer and Reflection

For your reflection and prayer, you may wish to use Joseph as a mirror. Reread Matthew 1 and 2. List Joseph's qualities afresh, as if he were new to you. Then use your list as a measure for yourself. What would you have done in his place?

Make your discoveries into prayer. You may give them to Joseph himself if you like—the communion of saints is real.

Remember to thank God, who became both foster Son and divine Father to Joseph—and who is willing to be both to you as well.

CHAPTER THREE

The Christmas Story in Luke

If you have just been immersed Matthew's story of Jesus' birth and turn now to Luke, you will sense immediately that you have entered a different atmosphere. Although these two Christian believers share some interests and a few vital traditions, they come from different backgrounds and write for different communities.

Once more, before you read the discussion, it is recommended that you read Luke 1 and 2 several times so you will be familiar with what Luke includes. Review the Appendix to help you.

Luke's and Matthew's Common Tradition

Luke writes much more than Matthew about events surrounding Jesus' birth. In fact, some of our dearest devotional traditions about Mary are found only in Luke. Her visit to

Elizabeth, the Canticle of Mary, the presentation of Jesus in the Temple—these mysteries of the rosary are written in Luke only. Furthermore, whereas Matthew says nothing about John the Baptist until he appears in the Judean desert (Matthew 3:1), Luke shows great interest in John's birth.

When we compare Luke 1 with Matthew, we find the following common points:

* Mary was betrothed to Joseph and was a virgin.
* Joseph was of the lineage of David.
* The expected son shall be named Jesus.
* Jesus was descended from David.
* Mary's child was conceived through the creative agency of the Holy Spirit.
* Therefore, Jesus is the Son of God (this exact title is found in Luke but not Matthew).

These common traditions were shared by both the writer of Luke in his mainly gentile Christian community and the writer of Matthew in his mainly Jewish Christian community. Although they can be listed quickly, they were essential traditions among the early Christians. Since both Matthew and Luke include them, explaining and enhancing them quite differently, we know they were vital to Christian memory.

Preparations for Jesus' Birth

Luke intends (1:1) to set out an ordered account of the traditions about Jesus, following careful investigation. It was a good thing to do, given the swirl of stories, opinions, and changes in the young Church of the 80s.

The first idea that Luke presents is that Jesus was not born into a vacuum but into a carefully prepared milieu. He describes the circumstances in the first chapter of his gospel with careful structure and multiple allusions to Old Testament stories.

Luke draws strong parallels between the prebirth story of John the Baptist and the prebirth story of Jesus. An angel announces each coming birth (to Zechariah, 1:11, and to Mary, 1:26). Then a response to the announcement enables more explanation (1:18 and 1:34). Action follows: Zechariah goes out to the people, then home (1:22-23); Mary visits Elizabeth (1:39-40). Two canticles are sung, both based on on Old Testament precedents: Mary sings at Elizabeth's home (1:46-55), and Zechariah sings after his son John's birth (1:68-79).

The birth of John is paralleled by the birth of Jesus in Luke 2.

The Birth Announcements
Luke 1:5-38

Luke's account of the preparation for John's birth is designed to demonstrate that John is in direct continuity with the Old Testament; more precisely, with the Israelite priesthood, being the son of a priest. Then Luke shows that Jesus' birth has the same elements of preparation, suggesting that Jesus is a further continuation of the same stream.

Luke accomplishes this by the skillful use of allusion—allusions his community would have recognized immediately but that are often lost on us because we do not know the Old Testament well enough.

The birth to a formerly barren woman older than the usual child-bearing age, for example, recalls two Old Testament women. Sarah was the wife of Abraham, the patriarch of Israel. The Lord had promised Abraham a multitude of descendants, but he had not even one son. Eventually, when Abraham and Sarah were quite old, Isaac was born to them. You may compare the stories in Genesis 18:9-15 and 21:1-7 with Luke 1:7, 24-25.

Then there was Hannah, who was told by a priest that in answer to her fervent prayers she would have a son. Hannah promised that this son would be dedicated to the Lord. When he was born, he was named Samuel (1 Samuel 1:1-28).

Both Isaac and Samuel were children of God's special notice and promise. Therefore, Luke implies, the two sons, John and Jesus, were likewise sent from God for special purposes. Therefore, they are trustworthy. Moreover, since Sarah and Abraham and Hannah lived before the complexities of Jewish law developed, they link gentile believers with the ancient plan of God.

The Responses and the Signs

The angel Gabriel comes to Zechariah, the priest, and to Mary, the virgin. Sons are promised. Zechariah's wife is barren; Mary has had no relations with a man. They both respond to the angel with questions—a standard reaction to angelic messages wherever they appear in the Old Testament. No one ever seemed to accept an angel's words without puzzlement over something.

The point in both stories is *not* primarily the psychology of Zechariah or Mary. We simply cannot know much about what each one felt inwardly at that moment. Their questions are similar, however. They give Luke an opportunity to tell *the reader* more about John, more about Jesus and their purposes in the divine plan. The device Luke uses here is like that of a playwright who needs to inform the audience of certain things, so he has the characters ask questions.

Luke's report of the angel's words about John recalls the prophetic tradition—thus the reference to Elijah. You may find a close reference in Malachi 3:24. Compare it to Luke 1:17. You will see that John's purpose continues the purposes of Old Testament prophecies: to bring people to repentance, to return people to God. This purpose vividly pervades John's adult ministry.

Jesus' purpose is greater. He will be the divine Son, who will establish an eternal kingdom (Luke 1:32-33). He will fulfill all that the ancient plan of God intended, incorporating the Old Testament promises and giving them totally new dimension because he is not only a prophet but the "Son of God."

After Gabriel's explanations to Zechariah and to Mary, each is given a sign. Signs, too, appear in Old Testament angelic messages. Zechariah cannot speak, and his wife's pregnancy becomes the divine sign to Mary.

After the announcement, Zechariah goes out to the people in the Temple courtyard as usual for the ritual he was to have performed—but he cannot bless them because he is mute.

Then Zechariah goes home.

Mary sets out to visit Elizabeth.

Living the Announcement Stories

Let's consider the pattern in the announcement stories. The messenger of the Lord comes unbidden and unexpected by the recipients of the divine message. The initiative is divine, not human. So it is with us as well. However much we may *feel* as if we have to beg before God acts, it is never the reality. God's Spirit stirs up our hearts to beg if it is something God wants us to experience.

If we fully assimilate the understanding that God takes all the valuable initiative, how might we want to live?

Alertly! Not that we expect to see an angel with wings and halo around every corner. We would surely trip over ourselves if that happened. Yet messengers can—and do—show up anywhere, anytime. God pours out communications to us constantly, only we miss them most of the time.

When waiting for the answer to a question that concerns you deeply, what is your attitude? Think about that for a moment. Remember how you listened for a friend to answer the last time you deeply wanted to know something. As someone said, when you want it enough, even the shapes of clouds can be God's messengers. But if you're not looking and listening, you may not notice the shapes of clouds!

Alertness for God's communications means cultivating an interest in everything. If we did that, however, we would certainly learn more and parade our own opinions less. We would find life spicier, too. Everything and everyone could become our teacher and our enjoyment if we ourselves had open, attentive hearts.

How do you do this?

You can begin every morning, while still in the comfort of a warm bed, by reminding yourself, *Today might bring a message from the Lord. I want to be alert and interested so I will hear it.* Then turn the self-reminder into a prayer. Get the help that is available! Right in that every moment, picture yourself being genuinely interested in everything. Gradually, your capacity will open.

If you are habitually bored or if you require large amounts of stimulation to "get" your interest, this effort will feel artificial at first. That's okay. All new attitudes feel awkward at first. If it is something good you want to cultivate, like habitual attentiveness to God throughout daily life, then help yourself by practicing what you want to become. You will become more aware of God's presence within you. Soon you will not miss as many tiny angels as you used to.

From both Zechariah and Mary, we learn that it's okay to ask questions. Even when our motives for questions are mixed—as they often are—we should be bold and ask God for what we want, be it knowledge, changes, favors, or something else. Even disbelief, when honestly expressed, can draw the grace of God, peculiar as that sounds. How often one who challenges God, like Zechariah, gets the strongest and most unmistakable response!

Too often we miss out on deeper understanding and closer experience of God because we do not ask. God always wants to give more than we are ready to receive, so asking our honest questions opens us to a flood of mercy and goodness, just as it did for Zechariah (in the end!) and for Mary.

Finally, let's open ourselves to the larger concern of Luke's announcement stories. Luke wanted people to know that these births were a continuation of the divine design, ancient in the earth, but being opened to fulfillment at the right time. We, too, are in the stream of God's grand design. We know it because Luke meant these stories for Gentiles—all of us.

If we stand consciously in God's design, what can really "go everything is in God's hands and that it will all come out for the good of our relationship with God? John is sent to turn people back to God; Jesus is sent to establish the kingdom of God (which later in Luke Jesus says is within us). By these announcements, not only Zechariah and Elizabeth and Mary and Joseph are given good news. We, too, are given good news: that all is in God's hands and that we may live close to God if we wish.

So after the drama is over, the questions raised, the attitudes changed, what then? Then, "thank you, thank you, thank you."

Digression:
The Immaculate Conception

Every December 8 at Mass, we hear the announcement of Gabriel to Mary read as the gospel. Many people confuse this announcement with the Immaculate Conception. A brief explanation here may clear up this confusion.

The doctrine of the Immaculate Conception does not refer to Jesus' being conceived in Mary's womb. It refers to Mary's being conceived in her mother's womb. Further, it has nothing to do with the idea of a nonsexual conception. The Church has never implied that Mary's mother was a virgin. The word *immaculate* as used here does not refer to sex at all, but to essential human nature.

This gospel reading is chosen because of the angel's greeting to Mary, calling her "full of grace." Theologians have taught that the only way a person can be full of grace is to be empty of original sin. So the Immaculate Conception means that from the moment of her conception Mary was protected and preserved from the original sin that haunts the rest of us so that she would be a totally pure vessel to receive God's Son.

Mary at Elizabeth's
Luke 1:39-45

Mary knows Elizabeth's secret—and knows it has divine meaning. Now, thanks to the baby in her womb, Elizabeth recognizes Mary's secret. The result is mutual awe at God's works and great joy.

The wonder of God's works! The joy that we human beings experience in the presence and work of God! These themes fill the Old Testament when God acts anew, and they are traceable especially through Luke's writings.

This scene, along with other details of Luke's birth stories, could not have been known by anyone except Mary and Elizabeth. Over the years, in order to "save" Luke's historical accuracy, the notion developed that Luke had sat at Mary's feet and taken notes.

It's a beautiful picture, but as biblical scholarship developed, it seemed more and more unlikely. Of course, there is no proof either way, but the weight of evidence suggests that Luke composed his birth stories from a variety of sources and reflections, probably not including Mary's memories.

Regardless of where Luke got his initial idea, the deepest source of meaning for us is to be found in what he did with what he had. What does Luke accomplish in his meeting of the two mothers-to-be?

First, Elizabeth blesses Mary. The form of her blessing appears often in the Old Testament, so once again we hear the Old Testament preparing for and rejoicing in the coming of Jesus. Mary and Elizabeth are part of the divine design.

Then Luke says, through Elizabeth, that Mary has believed the word of the Lord. Here Luke has begun to do something special with Mary: namely, to portray her as an ideal disciple of Jesus. This portrait can be traced all through the Gospel of Luke. It begins here in the birth stories, Luke's mini-gospel.

Mary has remained the ideal disciple ever since, because she has believed what has been said to her by the Lord's messenger and then she has acted. She shows trust and obedience, the core of discipleship.

The scene between Mary and Elizabeth suggests also that John's and Jesus' missions are related to each other and that John rejoices already in Jesus' coming—in the coming of the One who is superior to him. A pronouncement of the superiority of Jesus to John was likely necessary for a while. Both John and Jesus had disciples who were intensely loyal to their teacher. At some point, we think conflicts between the groups may have arisen, because all the gospels have treated the John-Jesus connection quite carefully.

Luke shows that John serves God by rejoicing in Jesus, just as Elizabeth rejoices in Mary's faith. Can we not also serve God by rejoicing in Jesus?

Living the Visit of Elizabeth and Mary

Obedience to the angel's hint (the sign) has brought Mary to Elizabeth. It is the occasion for great rejoicing. Of course, Luke's purpose is not especially to make examples of these women but to use their characters to proclaim the coming of Jesus in all its wonder. Nevertheless, Scripture offers more than one level of meaning, even here.

These two women have both received wonderful gifts from God, totally unexpected. Because we are so focused on Mary, Elizabeth is often ignored here. But she is a great example for us. She rejoices in what the Lord has done *for Mary*. She sees that Mary is greater than herself ("mother of my Lord"), and she is filled with delight over Mary—for Mary. Hers was a generous heart.

How generous are we? Are we truly happy for another's good fortune, or is our feeling colored with envy? When that person already seems to have more than we do, can we still rejoice in the new goodness? Or does our heart secretly wonder why that person who already has so much should get yet more?

Here's a test question. How would you feel if your next-door neighbor, who has an easier life than yours, won the lottery? Would you be able to give thanks to God for the great benefit to your neighbor?

A generous heart that is utterly free from envy is not too common. It requires an inner contentment with the gifts God has given to oneself and an appreciation of all gifts given to anyone else. It requires a certain humility and gratitude within one's own being. The rewards of such heartfelt generosity are found in a warm contentment at the core of one's being. It is good.

How to develop it? Practice, first of all. Do rejoice over everything good that happens to any and all around you. It doesn't have to be only those you know; in fact, for some it will be easier to start at a little distance from one's own life. Just be glad over every bit of goodness you see anywhere. Then express your gladness!

When you know the people involved, congratulate them, say you are happy for them, send cards and flowers—whatever expression comes easiest for you. Check your heart for envy. If you see it there, even a twinge, take it to God in prayer. Ask the Lord to remove it forever.

Warning: such a request will be fully answered, but in order for it to happen, you may have to experience envy very strongly one last time. If you don't squelch it but bear it with your inner focus of the Lord, it will be lifted away for good.

The Canticles
Luke 1:46-79

The Canticle of Mary is doubtless one of the most beloved prayers in all Christian history. It is beautiful, and it is indissolubly connected with our devotion to the Mother of Jesus. Still, we may not have it sink into our heart's understanding.

Zechariah's Canticle is almost equally loved. Both canticles appear daily in the Office of the Hours, traditionally chanted in religious communities. This one, too, we may not have considered carefully.

What has Luke done here?

Scholars usually (not always) think that Luke made use of

hymns that were already in Christian circulation. Each canticle combines shorter quotations from a number of Old Testament passages. The singing of a canticle in joy is like certain Old Testament figures (Hannah, for example, in 1 Samuel 2:1-10 and Judith 16:1-17).

The canticles in Luke do not fit exactly the circumstances of their respective singers. But their attitude, their general understanding of God and human relationships with God, is consistent with the experience of early Christians—and Christians ever since.

Living the Canticles

An outstanding characteristic of these two hymns is that they both give total credit to God for something wonderful that has happened in individual human experience.

What a splendid characteristic!

We humans tend to think that *we* do whatever is done, that our accomplishments are *ours*, and that we let God pinch hit when we get too tired or confused. God may *allow* us to think that, but it is far from the truth of life.

The truth is revealed in these canticles. Whatever happens that is good, that sparks joy in the heart, has its source in the action of God *right in the middle of our lives.* So whenever anything good happens, whether we think we did it or whether it was unexpected, we align ourselves to the truth by giving the credit to God.

This is no pious invention. Would we even exist without God? Would we have a single ability without God? Would any action, any idea, any result, be possible without God? No.

Yet how often we forget the One who is the source of all that we value, all that we do, all that we are. The canticles show that we can rejoice in God for every goodness, every pleasure, every gift. It is all the Lord's doing. We are only receivers—but what a joyful position that is when we let go of our egocentric determination to "do it myself."

If we want to live the canticles, we will rejoice daily, hourly, in everything that God gives, beginning with life itself.

The Birth of Jesus
Luke 2:1-7

Considering how Christians over the years have embroidered the story of Jesus' birth, Luke 2 seems quite simple when it is read afresh. Try it now. Read Luke 2:1-7 as if it were brand new to you.

As you read, notice particularly the following points.

1. Mary and Joseph come from Nazareth to Bethlehem. You will recall that this is different from Matthew's version.

2. While there, Mary has her baby son.

3. She wrapped the baby, like every mother did, and laid him in a manger because the inn had no place for them.

What is not here? There is no mention of the innkeeper, nothing further about a cave or a stable, nothing about the manner of the birth. All these ideas are later devotional reflections and are separate from the gospel. Perhaps one point could set us at rest about the inn—and the poor imaginary innkeeper.

Inns at that time were hardly private places like today's motels. They were often a large open area. As many travelers as could squeeze in laid their sleeping mats in the central part of the space. There were no partitions. Around the outside was a lower area, like a surrounding aisle, where the animals were bedded for the night: donkeys or camels or whatever the travelers were using. On one side, some open inns had a small roofed area for bad weather. It must have been total chaos. Hardly a fit place to have a baby!

Since the Greek term for *room* can also mean *place*, some commentators think Luke is saying that the inn was no place for them. We simply don't know what Luke really meant here.

Luke actually describes the birth of Jesus quite basically and simply. The birth is rooted in real history by its connections with the times and actions of known rulers—even though the dates don't exactly match other historical sources. Luke establishes that Jesus was born in Bethlehem—known Christian tradition, connected with the expectation of the Messiah (just as in Matthew). The swaddling clothes suggest that Jesus was a very ordinary physical baby, just as human as any other. They and the manger provide a sign for the shepherds in the next scene.

Living the Birth Scene

The poignancy of the Christmas scene over the years has been that Jesus—so great a being—had so simple and ordinary a birthplace. Again and again, we have asked ourselves if our own ordinary heart can be a birthplace for the Lord. Many might be honestly inclined to answer, "No, my heart is too small or it's too weak or it's too inadequate for Jesus to dwell there."

Perhaps that is one reason for Jesus' birth as a real baby: even a small or inadequate heart has room for a baby, does it not? If we are willing to let the baby Jesus be born in our heart, surely our heart will expand and grow stronger as Jesus grows within us.

When a baby is born, it inspires awe, but even more, a spontaneous and uncomplicated kind of love. The heart goes soft. The mind pauses in its racing. A smile appears. Joy arises.

All these natural responses are forms of love—love without need, without expectations. It is exactly the love that *is* God. If we could live every moment in that easy, contemplative, simple love for a tiny baby, we would be at one with the Lord already. So let us allow our heart to open at the memory of Mary's son, the human baby, the Lord of all.

Praying the Birth Scene

In your quiet solitude, let your mind relax. Keep this prayer as simple as Luke's scene is. Leave all the traditions and familiar reflections aside for this prayer time. Let go of all the paintings you've seen, all the imaginative ideas of how it might have been. Breathe easily. Be comfortable.

When you are totally at ease, turn your attention ever so gently to the space in your heart. There allow a simple image of a well-wrapped baby to appear. It is Jesus. He is just a baby. Allow your heart to be the place where this baby rests. Attend to him, nothing more. Welcome whatever arises in your heart. Stay with it as long as you are able. Just be with this baby.

After a while, the experience will close of itself. Let it go. Give thanks for this new or renewed birth of Jesus in your own being. Believe in it. It will begin—or begin again—a new life deep in your heart, where the Lord desires to dwell.

The Shepherds
Luke 2:15-21

The most amazing events are told so simply, so directly. Who has not tried to imagine what it was like on that dark hillside when the sky was alight with angels and glory? But Luke's deeper interests are not primarily in the drama.

Why shepherds? Again, we look to the Old Testament and find interesting connections. Moses was a shepherd for many years before God revealed himself to him in the burning bush (Exodus 3:1-6). David was a shepherd as a youth, long before he became king. Bethlehem was the city of David, the traditional ancestor of the Messiah.

Shepherds were not well regarded in Palestinian society. They lived rather outside usual social rules and sometimes were marauders as well. In addition to the reminder that Jesus was descended from a shepherd, there may be here a suggestion that these shepherds represent the "outsiders" who are included in Jesus' purposes. Luke says the joy of this birth will be for "*all* the people," not just for the well placed or the socially acceptable. The rest of Luke's Gospel also shows interest in the lowly and the unacceptable—who are utterly acceptable to Jesus.

So here, too, the birth story is a gospel in miniature. The shepherds receive the whole proclamation of the joyful news: "A savior has been born for *you* who is Messiah and Lord" (Luke 2:11). And then all heaven bursts into rejoicing.

We see in the shepherds the same pattern already noted in Joseph and in Mary. They receive an angelic announcement, they are frightened or puzzled, they are told "Do not be afraid" (Luke 2:10), they are given a sign. Then the shepherds, too, act on what they have been told: they hurry to see this baby, swaddled and in a manger. They tell what they have seen and heard. They rejoice and praise God. They leave and are not mentioned again.

Living With the Shepherds

To the shepherds the angel said that the birth of Jesus is for great joy in all people—so great a joy that amazing events occur around this birth. Reality is bursting with delight over the coming of Jesus!

Compared to that, how dull we often allow our Christian faith to become. It's as if we've heard it all innumerable times and the repetition does nothing for us.

Yet this is true only for the nominal Christian, the decent citizen who has not opened the heart to genuine Christian experience.

When you have an experience that is life-stirring and touches your very soul, don't you just love to tell it again and again, even if only to yourself? When a friend has a wonderful experience and shares it with you, isn't it a joy when she or he tells it again later in your hearing? Stories of real experience, our own or those of others, are repeated with love and delight. They continue to mean something to us and to all who hear and love us. Don't you delight in knowing what comes next?

The repetition of the stories about Jesus' birth will mean something every time we hear them *if* we have allowed the Lord to be born in our own heart, our own life. Otherwise, it's just information we already have. If that is the way these stories seem to you, you may take it as an indication that your experience of the Lord can bear deepening.

Outwardly dramatic events may or may not be given to us. But when Christ enters our life fully, *real* transformation begins. Then that moment of the Lord's birth becomes his birth *to* us and will be significant to us forever.

If transformation begins, we, too, will tell what we have seen and heard. We, too, will be amazed at the wonders that occur in us and in our circumstances.

A wonderful thing about living truth: no matter how often we have heard it in words, it is fresh and new and astonishing when it becomes our individual experience. Jesus is truth, and when we welcome him into us, boredom is gone forever and repetition only savors the whole splendor once again.

Living with the shepherds is mostly a matter of allowing the Lord into our daily perspective, our regular life. It is as simple and as world-shaking as that.

It can begin in a myriad of ways. You can ask for it; open to it. You can begin to act on what you know, now more deeply and attentively, because you really want the Lord within your heart. You can set time for daily prayer and emphasize self-offering in obedience. You can soak in the gospels. You can look within yourself and find the spot that seems most blocked; pray for its removal so that you may experience the birth of Jesus every day and with it the joy that is meant by God for all people.

Whatever you do, if it is sincere and if you persevere, you can count on the result: Jesus' birth will no longer be mere information but your own vital experience.

Jesus' Naming and Presentation to the Lord
Luke 2:22-38

By writing about Jesus' circumcision and naming, Luke places Jesus firmly within the Jewish law: all baby boys were circumcised eight days after their birth. With the naming of this baby *Jesus*, Gabriel's instructions to Mary were followed. Notice that no mention is made of Joseph or Mary in this incident. Rather, the name is simply given.

In Luke's account of the presentation of Jesus in the Temple, there are some details that don't quite match Jewish law. Taken together they indicate that Luke was not Jewish in background. Still, Mary and Joseph presented their firstborn to the Lord according to Jewish tradition and law and presented a sacrifice as all parents did. (Not all parents went to the Temple, however; most would have made their offering in a local synagogue.) This places Jesus once again in the mainstream of Judaic tradition.

In the presentation story, we meet Simeon and Anna, both elderly and of long and proven devotion to the Lord, both close to God. In their recognition of Jesus as savior and their response to him, Jesus is explicitly proclaimed to the world. Jesus will be salvation and light for all, the "glory of Israel" and revelation to the Gentiles (Luke 2:30-32).

Two points in Luke's Gospel parallel emphases in Matthew: that Jesus is for Jew and Gentile alike (Matthew's Gentiles are the magi, you will recall) and that some will welcome and adore Jesus and others (like Herod) will reject him (Luke 2:24). No matter how these stories came to the gospel writers, it is significant that Matthew and Luke both recognize that response to Jesus will always be divided.

Of course, they write from hindsight, yet there is more to it than that. By building these two contrasting responses into the Infancy Narratives, the two writers not only reflect what did happen but affirm that it was so intended by God from the very beginning. Christians have long understood that Jesus' death was no accident, that it was part of the redemptive design of God. Here in the birth stories is the same assertion. As mysterious as it may seem, Jesus' birth, life, disciples, death, and resurrection were designed from the beginning. That is the reason for the infancy stories.

Living the Presentation

Mary and Joseph were participants in a large drama of salvation. It had worldwide import. Yet, even knowing they were part of God's long-awaited fulfillment of ancient prophecies, they did not depart from the customs of their own faith.

They did not assume that they were somehow special and therefore exempt from living as their faith required. They claimed nothing for themselves but simply followed the Law.

They were, Luke says, "amazed at what was said about [Jesus]" (Luke 2:33). It fits with Luke's account about Mary at the end of the shepherds' scene: she "kept all these things, reflecting on them in her heart" (Luke 2:19).

We probably cannot rightfully speculate beyond the scriptural words about the thoughts of Mary and Joseph as they went through all these events. The stories are not meant for that. Yet their example offers food for reflection.

Mary and Joseph are righteous people, which puts them in firm standing in their own traditional faith. Thus, they keep the Jewish law, obedient to its prescriptions. They did the right thing according to the highest understanding they had, the traditions of their ancestors. They did not arrogate to themselves any particular credit, and they especially did not put themselves above the Law because of Jesus. They were equally obedient both to their roots and to the action of God in their lives.

Mary, according to Luke, goes a step further. Luke readies the reader to see in her a devoted disciple of Jesus when he becomes publicly active. (Joseph was apparently no longer alive then.) Her heart-full reflection on events shows this propensity in the beginning. Luke affirms that Mary's discipleship belongs to God's design. As Mary was "full of grace," she was capable of full discipleship as well.

So in our living of these examples, our pattern can be the same. No matter how special our lives may seem to us as individuals, we, too, do well to keep the traditions of our Christian ancestors. We do well to ponder the events of our lives in the light of our Christian discipleship. No matter what we find, we dare not put ourselves beyond the reach of Christian requirements.

Those requirements are not always totally clear in today's world. Controversy seems to rule on many issues that affect decisions in our daily lives. We need, therefore, to seek the foundation of Christianity to be able to determine our Christian responsibilities. We need to ponder long and deeply, as Mary did. We need to let Jesus be born to us.

If we are sincere about our search, we will give it time, energy, attention, prayer. We can begin with prayer. We can offer ourselves to God for God's purposes, ready to obey what we are given, ready to do what we know to do. God does respond, and the way will be shown to every truly searching heart—though it may mean a rending of our expectations, even as Zechariah's life was totally changed by his participation in God's design.

A second step available to all is the study of the Scriptures, especially all the gospels. Sometimes Christians get so involved in the life of Jesus or in their worship of him as Lord that we forget to immerse ourselves in his teachings. But mere fascination with Jesus, no matter what we believe *about* him, is not enough. We do better to become acquainted with his teachings firsthand. Study of Jesus' teachings in the gospels is indispensable to anyone who desires full discipleship. We do best to obey them, because only in the living of Jesus' teachings can we come to full understanding. Only in the living of the truth is our pondering fulfilled.

Return to Nazareth

In Luke's version, all the amazing events around Jesus' birth happened to Mary and Joseph far from home. But they did not stay in Bethlehem or try to live near the Temple. They simply went home to raise the child entrusted to their love. Luke says that Jesus grew and became strong and wise and lived in the favor of God.

If Jesus is our Lord, he is all the more our exemplar. Have

you ever made a conscious, deliberate decision to grow strong, to seek wisdom, to live so that God's favor will be yours? Often we take for granted the most amazing things! Doesn't life just give us those qualities if we live long enough?

No, not for sure. Besides, a life lived by conscious choice to follow Jesus in growth is qualitatively quite different from a life that just wanders along in the decency of going to church and being reasonably good. Those things are not bad. They are just far less than Jesus offers to his real disciples.

Jesus offers us the possibility of being like him. That is why he came as a baby and grew to manhood, why he taught, and why he died. Let's take that same course in following him. Let's begin—again and again if need be—to take him into our hearts as a baby, amid all the wonders we have permanently associated with his birth. Let's encourage that baby to grow in us just as surely and magnificently as he grew in Nazareth. Let's allow it to happen within us so that the growth will be truly ours. Let's pray constantly that every day of our life will be a step toward the end of the gospel begun at his birth: the end that is resurrection, fullness of being in God.

CHAPTER FOUR

The Prologue to John's Gospel

The Gospel of John was written down in the A.D. 90s, perhaps ten years after Matthew and Luke. As is immediately apparent to all attentive readers, John is told from a very different perspective than Matthew or Luke. Although they share many traditions, there is no evidence that the writer of John had ever seen either the Gospel of Mark (on which Matthew and Luke depend heavily) or Matthew or Luke.

John 21:24 does claim that the gospel depends on an eyewitness, which scholars think means that this eyewitness (perhaps John the apostle) headed a community of Christians within which the gospel was formed. Even so, this gospel bears within it the fruits of some sixty years of Christian experience after the Resurrection.

In Chapter One, it was explained that the early Christians

grew in their understanding of who Jesus was. Matthew and Luke reflect awareness that Jesus was Son of God from birth. There was one more step, expressed in John's Gospel: Jesus was the *eternal* Son of God. John's is the highest understanding of all.

The Prologue
John 1:1-18

John, of course, tells no birth stories as such. This gospel begins with the essential meaning of Jesus: who he was and what he gave his followers in their own experience. John expresses some of the highest *ideas* in the New Testament. They can seem quite abstract, requiring considerable rational explanation. However, let us never lose sight of the truth that for John the ideas *came after and were secondary to the experience of Jesus in the Christian heart and life*. John writes to invite—to urge—all others to enter into that same experience. Only then will the ideas be fully comprehended.

Open your Bible and read John 1:1-18. Whether this passage was an early Christian hymn or was composed by John is disputed and cannot be known with certainty. Regardless, it is one of the most glorious passages for prayer in the whole Scripture.

Before you take it to prayer, here is a brief review of some meanings John has drawn from his experience.

In John 1:1-5, the Word is identified with God from the beginning of all. The Word is the eternal creative word of God, existing before all time. The Word was no different from God, yet through the Word everything was created. In this divine Word is the source of all life, and life is light for human beings.

Recall that in Genesis 1, God creates *light* before the sun is created. Light is not merely physical light but inner light, the light of God, the kind of light we mean when we say someone has been "enlightened." It is like essential, universal energy—and was a direct creation of the Word itself, who was God.

Now look at John 1:9-14. John affirms that this true, enlightening light was coming into the world and was in the world, but was unrecognized.

The lack of recognition has a double meaning (at least). It refers historically to the Jewish people, who specially belonged to God but who did not recognize God in Jesus. More deeply, it refers to the divine Word and Light, which is always in the world and generally unseen by most people. God and Word never have been separate from the world: the world was created through the Word; it has always existed and has always been here. But, John affirms, it has remained largely unknown.

It remained unknown, that is, until "the Word became flesh" in Jesus Christ. Then the grace and glory, the truth and splendor, of revelation appeared in Jesus. Then the Word could be known, could be recognized, could be believed and accepted into the heart.

This is the culmination of Christian understanding of who Jesus was. Matthew and Luke showed clearly that Jesus was born of a virgin by the creative act of the Holy Spirit within her. For them, that stated definitely Jesus was born the Son of God. They do not make the next step—the step that after so many centuries of familiarity seems quite easy. John takes that final step: Jesus is the eternal Son, was always, will always be, because Jesus is the Word who is God.

John seconds, as it were, the affirmations of Matthew and Luke in 1:13: Jesus was not born by human decision nor in the usual way of human reproduction. He was born by God's act alone.

What Does It All Mean for Us?

It is as if John gathers the deepest and broadest early Christian experience and puts it into a single verse John 1:12. Jesus gave to those who accepted him "power to become children of God."

This was no abstraction for the early Christians. It was not even primarily a promise for life after death. It was their experience in this life: the experience intended by Jesus for all who wish it.

Today's Christians have often grown far away from first-hand knowledge of what it means to be a child of God. We are, it is often said, *all* children of God—meaning that we are all created by God. Yes, of course, we are. That is not what John means in this verse, however.

Today's Christians often take the phrase figuratively, to mean that God loves us as his own or some similar sentiment. Yes, of course, that is true as well. But it is not what John means, either.

What John is claiming was more commonly understood in the earliest days of Christian faith, long before the practice of infant baptism. In those days, baptism was a fully adult decision. Frequently, perhaps always at the very first, this decision followed on an experience so strong and joyful and loving that one could hardly do anything else but accept Jesus totally.

What did the early Christians understand by the phrase "child of God"? To them, it meant that every human being—you and I—through Jesus can become *by grace* what Jesus actually was from all eternity: Son of God.

Pause and reflect, right now: the eternal Son came in flesh, born of a human mother and named Jesus so that you and I can become what he was.

Where would the grace for such a transformation come from? It came from Jesus, the source of creation: "From his fullness we have all received, grace [upon] grace, because...grace and truth came through Jesus Christ" (John 1:16-17). It's like a circle. The Word eternally is and is one with God. The Word creates the world and human beings. The Word enters flesh so that all humans might see, know, and desire the glory of being a "child of God." The enfleshed Word, Jesus, gives the possibility and the power for that transformation. Then the human beings, one by one, enter into the same oneness with God.

This is the meaning and possibility brought to everyone by the Incarnation of the Lord. This is the reality we celebrate at Christmas. This is the foundation of all the Christmas stories and myths. Those stories are a springboard into appropriating Jesus and all he offers.

Christmas and Beyond: Living John's Prologue

If one wants to go forward into the essence of Christian possibility and become truly a child of God, the best beginning is in prayer.

In a retreat I once led, a nun wanted to spend a week of silence with the Gospel of John. She began with the Prologue, expecting to proceed through all twenty-one chapters during the course of the retreat. She spent the whole week praying the Prologue. When she left, she knew in every pore that she could become a child of God. She knew without doubt who Jesus was for her and the transformation he could create in her. Intense, uninterrupted prayer with the Prologue gave her—for the first time, she said—the core of Christian spiritual life.

If you need to, review the description of *lectio divina* on page 14. Taking John 1:1-18 as your selected Scripture passage, go to prayer in that way.

Plan to spend more than one session of prayer with John's Prologue. Do anything you can to help it saturate your heart, your mind, even your body. Copy it and put it up where you can read it again and again. Maybe you'll want to memorize it. Carry it around like a talisman and look at it whenever you have to wait at a red light, in a grocery line, or a doctor's waiting room.

There is endless depth in these verses. They can penetrate our being until they are truly a place where we meet the Lord. After years of working with the Prologue as scholar and Christian, a friend of mine says she still cannot read it aloud without weeping. Familiarity has only made it more beautiful as it increasingly expresses her own experience.

You can make it your experience, too, if you will. Jesus came for that—for you.

Where Do We Go From Here?

This brief look at the stories of Jesus' birth gives only a taste of what they can mean to us. Living with them and opening our heart and mind to more prayer and further study will allow them to continue to unfold in our living. They will deepen our understanding and whet our appetite for more of the Lord in our experience.

The birth stories are like beginning gospels. They reveal the significance of Jesus in miniature, similarly to his coming as a "mini" person, a baby. Since they are the beginning of the whole gospel story, the Church has placed them close to the beginning of the liturgical year.

So also the birth stories of Jesus can be a beginning—or a new beginning—for us. They can open us afresh to the possibilities of personal inner experience of Jesus as our Lord. They can begin or renew our whole relationship with God. They can simplify us, encourage us, strengthen us.

We have only to let them into our inner being. Then the possibilities open to our spiritual growth are infinite because the Lord is infinite. We can enter ever more fully into the life of God.

Shall we go?

Appendix

In Matthew Only

❈ Quoted references to the Old Testament

❈ Joseph's home is in Bethlehem

❈ The magi visit the baby Jesus

❈ Joseph, Mary, and the baby flee to Egypt

❈ The massacre of the infants in Bethlehem

❈ Return from Egypt to Judea, then to Nazareth

In Luke Only

❈ The angelic announcement to Zechariah

❈ The birth of John the Baptist

❈ Mary and Joseph's home in Nazareth

❈ The angelic announcement to Mary

❈ Mary's visit to Elizabeth

❈ The canticle of Mary

❈ The canticle of Zechariah

❈ The shepherds and the angels

❈ The circumcision of Jesus and the presentation in the Temple

❈ The return from Jerusalem to Nazareth

Common to Matthew and Luke

❋ Genealogy, though each one is different

❋ The birth of Jesus in Bethlehem

❋ Mary is a virgin when Jesus is born

❋ Jesus is conceived through the power of the Holy Spirit

❋ Jesus is the son of David, traced legally through Joseph

❋ An angel says that the baby will be named Jesus and that he will be the Savior

❋ Jesus grows up in Nazareth

More From Marilyn Gustin...

You Can Know God
Christian Spirituality for Daily Living
This book is written for anyone who is homesick for God. Every idea and every practice in it is a readiness exercise, because readers can experience God right where they are and know the Lord more directly in their ordinary lives. *$9.95*

How to Read and Pray the Parables
"This guide to personal growth and self-examination is written to be tasted in small bites and savored in extended concentration on the kernel of truth which surprises us each time we approach a parable." —Modern Liturgy. *$2.50*

How to Read and Pray the Gospels
Blending solid biblical scholarship with faith, Marilyn Gustin presents a guide to better understanding of the gospels for all Christians. Includes prayer suggestions, ideas for family Bible study, and questions for discussion. *$2.50*

Witness to the Light
Discovering the Spirit of John's Gospel
Marilyn Gustin unlocks the interior meaning of the Gospel of John and shows how this gospel is a "how-to" manual for reaching the ultimate Christian goal: full union with God. *$4.95*

Order from your local bookstore or write to
Liguori Publications
Box 060, Liguori, MO 63057-9999
(Please add $1 for postage and handling for orders under $5; $1.50 for orders over $5.)
For faster service call toll-free (800) 325-9521, ext. 060.
Please have Visa or MasterCard ready.